Matthew Clark

Most

Haunted

Exorcisms and Possessions

A Scary Journey in the Most Famous True Stories of Exorcisms and Demonic Possessions

Table of Contents

Introduction

Suppose you're into horror movies or scary stories. In that case, you'll know that the leading category in this niche is demon possession or Exorcism, in contrast to its counterpart, the zombie apocalypse, and related stories. They uniquely give you the chills that the other can't provide because of the mysterious intrigue attached to every scene and that most movies are adopted from true-life stories.

Before then, let's look at what possession and Exorcism are all about. Either it's a family or bloodline curse, you piss a voodoo priest off, or some loose spirit or demon was just having a bad day and decided to transfer aggression on whoever crossed its path. It all boils down to being possessed or taken control of by a mythical being or entity. During such periods, the victims may or may not lose consciousness and have little or no control of their bodies or coordination functions.

According to a Vatican-approved exorcist, the different signs of possession include; aversion to the sacred; so a person walks in this Church and can't look at a crucifix, and their eyes are, you only see the whites of their eyes. Another would be knowledge of hidden things, where the demon will begin to tell you something about yourself that the person would have no way of knowing. It would be followed by possessing a kind of excessive physical strength they don't normally possess. Eventually, epileptic-like seizures on a person's face and the movement of their arms and legs in a way where they lose complete control. So, if you are or know of someone experiencing such, and the person has tried medical approaches, it could be that the person is possessed.

On the other hand, Exorcism is the act of removing or expelling said demon or possessing an individual by using books, texts, and other materials that are believed to eliminate said demons.

The following cases are some real-life cases of possessions and exorcisms that have happened in the past, leaving places involved haunted and also sending chills down your spine.

1.The Exorcism of Anneliese Michel

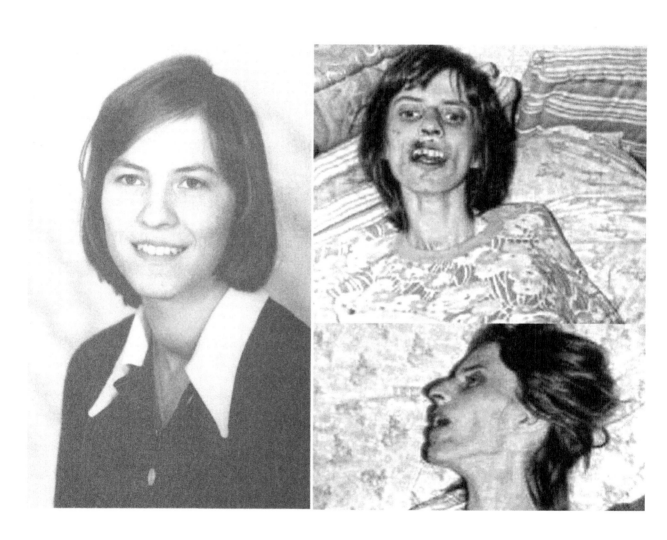

Anna Elisabeth "Anneliese" Michel (September 21, 1952 – July 1, 1976) was a German lady who died after undergoing 67 Catholic exorcism rituals in the year leading up to her death. Her parents and Priest were found guilty of negligent homicide when she died of hunger. She had been diagnosed with epileptic psychosis (temporal lobe epilepsy) and had a history of ineffective psychiatric therapy.

Anneliese Michel was born in 1952 in the small German town of Klingenberg and was raised as a strict Catholic. She was considered bright and charming. Anneliese had her first incident of falling unconscious when she was 16 years old, in September 1968. She also felt like something was pushing down on her chest, pinning her to her bed later that night. A similar incident occurred 11 months later, in August 1969. Anneliese's mother took her to their family doctor, Dr. Vogt, and a neurologist, Dr. Luthy, who examined her and even conducted an electroencephalogram, or EEG, a brain scan, discovered nothing wrong. They speculated that it could be a seizure of some sort.

Anneliese had two more similar incidents over the next three years, for which she has prescribed two medications: an anticonvulsant and an anti-seizure medicine called Dilantin. By the age of 20, she had developed an intolerance for many religious artifacts and heard voices. Despite medicine, her illness worsened, and she became suicidal and exhibited other symptoms for which she was treated. After five years of taking psychiatric drugs, Michel and her family became afraid a demon-possessed failed to alleviate her symptoms.

Things began to take a bizarre turn in the spring of 1973. In her bedroom, Anneliese began to hear knocking sounds. It sounds that her sisters would also hear. Anneliese also claimed to have heard a voice telling her she was going to hell. Anneliese's mother was even more alarmed when she saw her daughter intensely staring at a statue of the Virgin Mary with "eyes became black, jet black, and her hands seemed to morph into thick paws with claws," according to her mother.

Anneliese recounted terrifying visions of a demon face haunting her in September 1973 during a neurology visit with Dr. Luthy and stated that she believed the Devil was inside her. She also reported smelling something like burning feces, an odor that several others around her also confirmed detecting. Around this time, Anneliese's mother told Dr. Luthy about the weird incidents, and he urged them to contact a Jesuit, according to Mrs. Michel, a remark that Dr. Luthy later denied. Anneliese visited with a Freudian psychiatrist in November 1973, who described her as a neurotic with potential epilepsy. Another physician discovered she had "epileptic tendencies" and switched her from Dilantin to Tegretol, a much harsher medicine.

Anneliese's bizarre conduct increased in July 1975. She didn't get much sleep and spent the night praying earnestly. She ate spiders and flies, and she even licked the pee off the floor. On the walls, she smashed rosaries, crucifixes, and sacred pictures. Anneliese also showed "near-superhuman strength," throwing her sister "like if she were a ragdoll," and amazingly, effortlessly squeezing an apple with one hand into "fragments erupted over the room." Also, a priest named Father Rodewyk, who was regarded as an expert on exorcisms by his colleagues, said that he was sure that Anneliese was possessed and that an exorcism on Anneliese was formally allowed after consultation with the bishop.

Whether or not this is true, the family looked for a priest, and they eventually found Father Alt. When they met the Priest Ernst Alt, he told them that she "didn't appear like an epileptic" and that he didn't notice her having seizures. Alt claimed she was possessed by a demon and pleaded with the local bishop to allow an exorcism. Bishop Josef Stangl allowed the Priest Arnold Renz permission to exorcise according to the Ritual Romanum of 1614 in September of the same year, albeit with strict confidentiality. On September 24, 1975, it was to be carried out by Father Renz, a priest. Father Renz performed the first exorcism rite, and he allowed part of the exorcism sessions to be recorded, resulting in 42 audio recordings of exorcisms.

The first session was held on September 24 by Renz. Michel started talking about "dying to atone for the wayward youth of the day and the apostate priests of the modern church." Her parents stopped seeing doctors and instead relied completely on exorcism rites at this point. Over ten months in 1975–1976, 67 exorcism sessions were performed, one or two each week, lasting up to four hours.

During her sessions, Anneliese identified Fleischmann as one of her demons, providing correct details about the real Fleischmann, a priest. He was expelled from the Church for poor behavior in the 1500s. Father Alt, who believed Anneliese would have no way of knowing Fleischmann, was taken aback by these revelations.

Anneliese's behavior escalated by May when she began slamming her head against the wall and biting herself and others to the point where her family had to bind her to protect her from injuring herself. Anneliese's condition exacerbated her refusal to eat, which she described as "not being permitted to eat." Even though she was fragile and presumably weighed less than 80 pounds, she showed incredible strength when people tried to confine her.

Anneliese's entire face was sunk in by June, and she refused to see a doctor despite having a high temperature. Anneliese had another exorcism on June 30 and merely said, "Please, absolve me." Her relatives went to her room the next morning and discovered her dead.

Despite seeking medical help early on, Anneliese ultimately refused to submit to medical treatment, as she and her family put their confidence in exorcisms for the cure. After 67 exorcisms, she died of malnutrition at the age of 23. At the time of her death, she weighed barely 68 pounds.

The case was taken to court, and her family members and the other parties involved were put on trial. The defense presented eyewitness testimony and formally submitted the recordings as possession evidence, an idea that the court never seemed to take seriously. The defense argued that Anneliese was allowed to refuse medical treatment because it was her legal right, even though the medical treatment could have included tranquilization, force-feeding, and electroshock therapy. All of this is presumably done against her will. Even a family friend, Thea Hein, testified that Anneliese reportedly "begged on her knees" for Hein not to suggest medical attention to anyone in 1976, a few months before her death. However, near the end, Father Alt sought medical assistance. On May 30, his friend Dr. Richard Roth visited Anneliese out of his scientific curiosity rather than a physician.

The prosecution claimed that Anneliese had epilepsy and psychosis and that her parents and two priests were responsible for her death by failing to intervene. According to two experts, they questioned Father Alt's credibility, claiming that he showed signs of schizophrenia. The prosecution also claimed that the medications given effectively suppressed epilepsy-like seizures and that this suppression evolved into "a delusional psychosis associated with epilepsy." They claimed that Anneliese's psychosis was aggravated by the exorcisms, which only served to fuel her fantasy.

It meant that Anneliese would go through periods of normal behavior in between exorcisms. Even though she would act possessed during exorcisms, it's unclear whether Anneliese's epilepsy-like seizures were suppressed by medication or if they went away on their own, even if her psychotic visions predate the alleged medical suppression.

In the end, the court sided with the prosecution, and the four defendants were sentenced to six months in prison, suspended for three years, and ordered to pay all court costs. The court ruled that Anneliese was incapable of making her own decisions and should have been forced to undergo medical treatment.

2.The Exorcism of Anna Ecklund

Ecklund's first awareness of a feeling of disgust toward religious objects began when he was 14 years old. When she was born in Marathon, Wisconsin, and was raised as a Catholic, she could not enter churches. Something unknown seemed to hold her back. Ecklund was possessed by demons when Riesinger arrived in 1912. Because she couldn't pray or go to Church, Anna Ecklund could not receive sacraments, even though she continued to have faith. With every step she took, she heard demonic spirits whispering urgently in her ear, urging her to do terrible things. Feeling that she was losing her mind, Anna despaired. The demons returned to their previous effort levels, according to Riesinger. According to the Catholic mythos, he believed that a demonic being possessed her, and seven of his demons accompanied him. Exorcism would be much more difficult if these beings could possess humans.

Riesinger was well aware of the stakes and the potential for an exorcism to cause problems. Following the first rite, rumors circulated that Anna had been possessed due to her father Jacob's incestuous advances or that her aunt Mina had used black magic as a witch. Riesinger sought advice from his friend, Reverend Joseph Steiger of St. Joseph's parish in Earling, Iowa, because the suffering woman's soul was on the line, and there was a risk of intense local backlash. They decided to take Anna to an isolated convent run by Franciscan Sisters in Earling to ensure privacy and protection. They started making preparations for the woman's Exorcism there.

After receiving permission from the Mother Superior, the reverends brought Anna to the convent on August 17, 1928. She hissed in aversion when she smelled food that had been blessed, and she could tell when holy water had been sprinkled ahead of time. Anna was bound to an iron bed for the first of three sessions the next day to prevent any dangerous behavior. Riesinger, who has years of experience, fully expected her to attack during the ceremony. He had the convent's strongest sisters on standby to assist him.

Nothing, however, had prepared the reverends for what was about to happen. Anna sank into a deep sleep with her eyes shut tight as they said the opening prayers. She then allegedly ripped through her restraints, leaped into the air, and clung to the wall above the room's door as they officially began the exorcism rite. Theophilus had the sisters drag Anna away from the wall and into the bed, restraining her even as she howled inhumanly until the end of the first session on August 26.

Over the next two sessions, Anna quickly deteriorated from September 13 to 20 and December 15 to 23. Despite eating less and less, she vomited inexplicably large amounts during the exorcisms. Tobacco leaves and other debris seemed to make up the majority of the vomit. Anna's body began to change and distort as the demons inside her changed and distort her body physically. Her head swelled and elongated, and her face became so disfigured that few people recognized her as the humble woman who had arrived at the convent. By the end, she was a pale, deathlike figure, her body emaciated, and her eyes are glowing like red embers.

Anna's behavior changed as the Exorcism progressed. In addition to the vomit, she began to produce an uncontrollable amount of urine and feces. Anna reacted angrily to the Priest's actions, foaming at the mouth whenever Riesinger said Latin blessings. Her body even swelled to twice its normal size on one occasion, making the sisters in the room wince in fear of the woman bursting. Anna spoke in languages she had never heard before and could recall the nuns' and priests' childhood sins. After a short period, several sisters requested to leave their home for a convent with fewer problems.

They couldn't be blamed, given Anna's ongoing transformation. Her soft voice often devolved into a guttural growl capable of making unimaginable noises.

Her body grew heavier, and she pressed so hard against the iron-wrought bed frame that it bent. Even while sleeping, she spoke in strange tongues, cursing God and verbally abusing anyone in the room. Anna could be brought back to her senses by blessed or holy objects, so there was still hope. The closer they got to evil Riesinger, Steiger, and the sisters, the longer they chased that hope. Anna listed several spirits within her when asked about them, with Beelzebub as their leader. She did, however, mention that she had been possessed by her father, Jacob, and his mistress, Mina, with the assistance of Lucifer himself.

The first Exorcism had failed, according to her, because Jacob and Mina continued to poison her food with cursed spices. The pair had been cursed and had now joined Anna's demon horde. "To bring her to despair so that she will commit suicide and hang herself!" said a voice claiming to be Judas Iscariot when asked what business the spirits had with her. The Exorcism would soon be over once the demons were identified. The final session began on December 23, 1928. Anna Ecklund collapsed on her bed after standing up and screaming at the top of her lungs. When Anna's screams reached a fever pitch, an unearthly stench filled the room, and she fell silent. She blinked open her eyes. Then, for the first time in months, she spoke in a clear voice. The Exorcism was completed after 23 days, and the evil had vanished.

Ecklund was able to live a relatively peaceful existence in the years that followed. Her true identity was kept hidden from the public. Reverend Steiger was a man who lived a full life. And as more people read Begone, Satan!, the book's popularity grows. Riesinger's popularity grew. He was well-known in the Catholic community before his death in 1941, and he was featured in Time magazine in 1936.

3.The Exorcism of Roland Doe

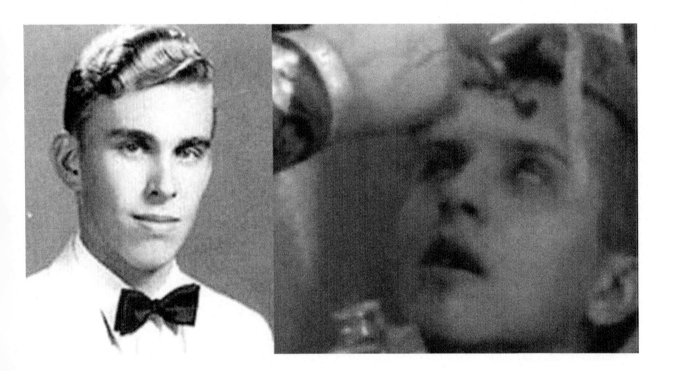

In 1949, Jesuit priests alleged they performed an exorcism in St. Louis on a boy, known pseudonymously as Roland Doe, after exhibiting signs of demonic possession after playing with an Ouija board. Roland was born into a Lutheran household in Germany. The family lived in Cottage City, Maryland, in the 1940s. Roland, according to Allen, was an only kid who relied on adults in his household for playmates, particularly his Aunt Harriet. When Roland displayed curiosity in the Ouija board, his aunt, who was a spiritualist, introduced him to it.

Before Exorcism, Roland often spoke in German and Italian dialects, which he had no prior knowledge of. During the Exorcism, Roland growled while exhibiting superhuman strength. The Exorcism was eventually performed when doctors could not find any medical explanation for the boy's actions and symptoms.

This story was presented in a documentary produced by the Catholic League and broadcast on CNN. However, the story is baseless, and few doctors even believed the story occurred. One doctor even stated that "It doesn't sound right. It sounds like a made-up story..."

Before becoming a Canon of St. Louis Cathedral, Fr. Richard Sipe interviewed one of the priests who performed the Exorcism, Frs Eugene Aull, and Roland Doe himself, and concluded that "I don't think [Roland] experienced evil spirits."

Was Roland Doe's Exorcism real or fabricated?

Despite being reported in various publications at the time and supported by several Jesuit priests and other witnesses, current skeptics have found numerous gaps in the account. What we do know is that a youngster from Cottage City, Maryland (not Mt. Rainier, Maryland, as many sources claimed), identified variously as Roland Doe and Robbie Manheim, was taken to St. Louis for treatment for troubling conduct.

Whether the disturbing behavior was caused by psychiatric disease, demonic possession, or a clever joke depends on who you believe. Many parts of the narrative, including where the youngster came from and whether he was first sent to Georgetown Hospital for treatment, proved incorrect.

While some of those could be dismissed as changes to protect the boy's identity, Opsasnick obtained quite different statements from witnesses and neighbors he interviewed.

The general agreement appears that Roland/Robbie was acting out due to emotional issues or a psychiatric episode, but nothing supernatural occurred. On the other hand, psychiatrists were more likely to see mental illness in the incidents they watched, whereas priests were more likely to see demonic possession.

There was at least one Exorcism done, according to diary reports kept by at least two priests who claim to have participated in the rituals: William S. Bowdern and Raymond J. Bishop. Both priests taught at St. Louis University, and the latter claims he found out about Roland via a classmate who happened to be the boy's cousin. Both were sure that they were in the presence of a demon in their accounts.

When author Thomas B. Allen, who published the book Possessed about Roland Doe's Exorcism, interviewed the third Priest in attendance, Thomas Halloran, he seemed to have concerns.

Where did Roland Doe's Exorcism take place?

Given the number of witnesses, it's likely that a ritual did take place in St. Louis in 1949. The boy's parents accompanied him from Maryland to Missouri, where he was treated at the university and then at The Alexian Brothers Hospital in a razed wing in 1978. The house Roland remained in with his family, on the other hand, is a popular tourist spot on Roanoke Drive and has been visited by many paranormal investigators, including the Ghost Adventures crew, over the years.

At least as of 2013, the youngster, whose name has never been revealed, appeared to be alive and in his 70s, living a regular life.

When Opsasnick found him (or thought he saw him), he didn't confirm or deny he was Roland Doe, but he made it obvious he didn't want to be interrogated about it. The priests who narrated the story have all passed away.

After the Exorcism

Following the Exorcism of "Roland Doe, his family relocated to the East. According to sources, Ronald married and established a family. He called his first child Michael after the saint who was thought to have saved his soul. Roland would be in his early 80s if he were still living today.

Following the Exorcism, the chamber at Alexian Brothers Hospital was boarded up and shut. The entire complex was demolished in 1978. After being abandoned in the 1960s, the family's home in Maryland is now an empty lot.

Experts think "Roland Doe's" true identity is Ronald Hunkeler. However, only one individual apparently knows for certain, the Priest.

4.David Berkowitz, Son of Sam Demonic Possession.

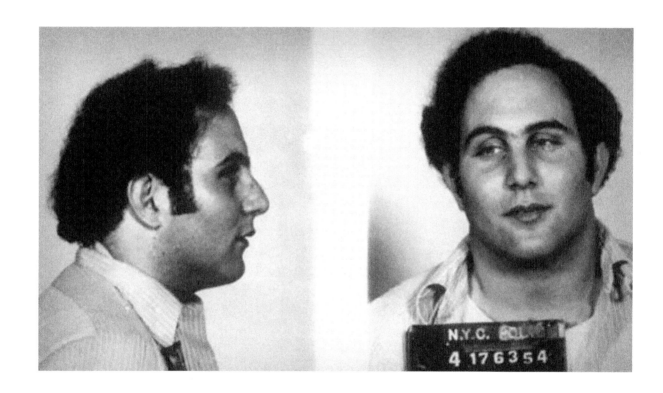

During the "Summer of Sam" in 1977, David Berkowitz shot, injured, and killed over ten people in New York City, New York. He was well-known and regarded as the personification of sin and evil. Serial killers may feel compelled to kill by an outside power larger than themselves, which can be both good and evil. These murders are performed in an attempt to fill or satisfy an emptiness in their lives, whether spiritual or not, and to overcome concerns, fears, loneliness, and insanity. David Berkowitz said that Satan drove him to conduct such heinous actions and that he was controlled and instructed to kill. He stated that his killings were not the issue but rather the way to defeating the demons that possessed him. He felt demonically possessed and sent notes marked with his tag the Son of Sam to the police and the news after his kills so that people would understand why he was doing this in the name of Satan.

David Background

David Berkowitz was raised in the Bronx by adoptive parents. He was shocked by the loss of his adopted mother from cancer in 1967, and he became increasingly isolated as a result. He entered the army in 1971 and served for three years, where he distinguished himself as a skilled marksman. He returned to New York in 1974 to work as a security guard. In 1975, his mental state worsened dramatically (he would later be diagnosed as a paranoid schizophrenic).

Feeling cut off from the rest of the world, he became an arsonist and ignited hundreds of fires in New York City without being apprehended. He began to hear voices of "demons" tormenting him and telling him to murder. On Christmas Eve 1975, he succumbed to his inner demons and badly injured 15-year-old Michelle Forman with a hunting knife.

He moved into a two-family home in Yonkers, a New York suburb, in January 1976. Berkowitz became persuaded that the German shepherd in the home and other neighboring dogs were possessed by devils who commanded him to murder attractive young ladies. During this period, one of the neighboring dogs was shot, most likely by Berkowitz. He began to perceive his neighbors as devils as well.

Berkowitz relocated to an apartment house in Yonkers in April, but his new residence also contained dogs. Berkowitz's next-door neighbor, retiree Sam Carr, owned a black Labrador dog named Harvey, whom he felt begged him to murder. He also saw Sam Carr as a strong demon and referred to him when he subsequently referred to himself as "Son of Sam."

His Attack

Berkowitz resigned from his position as a security guard on July 28, 1976. The next morning, he approached a parked automobile in the Bronx where two young ladies were conversing and fired five rounds into the vehicle with his .44 revolver. Donna Lauria, eighteen, was murdered instantaneously, and her companion Jody Valenti was injured. There were no motivations or leads in the shooting, according to police.

Berkowitz attacked again in the early hours of October 24, gravely injuring 20-year-old Carl Denaro as he sat in a vehicle in Queens, talking with a female acquaintance. On November 26, a little more than a month later, 16-year-old Donna DeMasi and 18-year-old Joanne Lomino were shot and badly injured on the street on their way home after a movie. Berkowitz fatally shot Christine Freund while she sat in a vehicle in Queens with her boyfriend on January 30, 1977. Police began to assume that a single person committed these crimes, but only a few bullets were discovered undamaged to back up their suspicions.

Virginia Voskerichian, a 19-year-old college student, was shot to death as she went home in Manhattan on March 8. A bullet was discovered undamaged, matching one discovered at the scene of Berkowitz's first murder. The New York Police Department reported the capture of a serial murderer, described as a Caucasian guy in his twenties with black hair and of average height and build.

To find the murderer, a huge squad of investigators known as the "Omega" task team was formed. Valentina Suriani, 18, and Alexander Esau, 20, were shot and murdered by the same pistol while they kissed in their parked automobile along the Hutchinson River Parkway on April 17. This time, the. The 44-caliber assassin left a message referring to himself as the Son of Sam.

Berkowitz shot Sam Carr's Labrador dog on April 29. He had already sent Mr. Carr an anonymous, threatening letter about the animal. The dog was rescued, and the Yonkers Police Department launched an investigation. Meanwhile, Berkowitz started writing strange messages to his neighbors and previous landlords. These people began to think Berkowitz was the Son of Sam and reported their concerns to local authorities. The Omega task team was alerted later, but the investigators had received hundreds of reports of Son of Sam "suspects" and were having difficulty filtering through all the dead ends.

The Son of Sam attacked again on June 26, injuring Judy Placido and Sal Lupo as they sat in their car after leaving a Queens disco. The public's fear of the rampaging serial murderer reached crisis proportions, and New York's nightclubs and restaurants witnessed a significant reduction in business. A scorching heatwave and a 25-hour blackout in mid-July only added to the angst. Berkowitz shot a young couple kissing in a parked car in Brooklyn on July 31, only two days after the anniversary of his first homicide. Stacy Moskowitz, twenty, was killed, and her boyfriend, Bobby Violante, lost his left eye and virtually all of his vision in his right eye.

A few days later, a key breakthrough in the case occurred when an eyewitness reported seeing a guy with what seemed to be a pistol minutes before the shots were fired in Brooklyn. Her information contributed to the creation of the first police sketch of Berkowitz. More importantly, she informed detectives that two police officers had issued parking fines on her street that night. Berkowitz's vehicle was finally discovered after a scan of issued tickets.

Simultaneously, Yonkers police looked into Berkowitz after he launched a harassment campaign against one of his neighbors. They alerted the Omega task group of their discoveries, convinced he was the Son of Sam. The Omega investigators eventually connected the dots, and David Berkowitz was apprehended while leaving his Yonkers home on August 10. He happily acknowledged to being Sam's son. He was carrying a semiautomatic weapon and said that he was on his way to conduct another murder. A .44-caliber revolver was also found.

There was some doubt regarding Berkowitz's mental capacity to stand trial, but on May 8, 1978, he dropped his insanity defense and pled guilty to the six murders. On the other hand, Berkowitz appeared to like the media attention his case was receiving, and he went on to sell his exclusive narrative rights to a publishing firm. This spurred New York state to enact the first of a countrywide series of so-called "Son of Sam laws," which direct the money earned by a criminal from selling their tale to a victims' compensation fund.

Berkowitz was causing harm and killing people because he believed it would release him from his possessions and obsessions. "I was once a bad guy, and I genuinely thought that Satan would come and free me," he says. He received six sentences ranging from 25 years to life in prison for the crime, which was the maximum penalty allowed at the time. He supposedly stated during his first year in prison in 1979 that he "created the Son of Sam stories so that if he ever got discovered, he could claim insanity in court." After a decade in prison, he adopted a new identity as the self-proclaimed "Son of Hope." Berkowitz believes he has been pardoned and redeemed, which means he believes he has finally overcome his demonic control. Since then, he has been denied parole. He is presently incarcerated in the Shawangunk Correctional Facility in upstate New York, where he is said to have converted to Christianity.

5.Carolyn Perron and the Perron Family

The Perron Family: father Roger, Mother Carolyn, and their five children, Andrea, Nancy, Christine, Cindy, and April, moved into the farmhouse they purchased in Harrisville, Rhode Island, in 1971. The farmhouse provided enough space for them to raise their five kids. They had no idea what would happen throughout the decade they stayed there. When they moved in, the former owners only gave them one piece of advice: "For the sake of your family, leave the lights on at night!" While they were perplexed by the comment at first, it wouldn't be long before they followed the advice.

The Perrons lived in the house for several years, gradually uncovering its history and the numerous prior residents who had died there. While their findings were bleak, Roger and Carolyn may have accepted the house's darker days if it hadn't been for the spirits that lingered in the house long after they died.

In the Winter of 1971, The Perron Family decided that a tranquil life in the country was in order. Roger and

Carolyn moved into a big, ten-bedroom mansion in Harrisville, Rhode Island, with their five kids. The mansion, known as The Old Arnold Estate, was completed in 1736 and lay on 200 acres of land. Almost soon, paranormal activity began. The girls became aware of a small guy roaming about the house. He frequently moved their toys around behind their backs, unnoticed. Carolyn, too, began to realize that someone or something was moving the broom. She would occasionally hear the sound of the broom's bristles scratching across the kitchen tile. When she went and returned, she would frequently discover a little amount of dirt in the center of the floor.

Another ghost gradually revealed itself to the Perron sisters. A guy with a crooked smile would emerge in the corners of their room, observing the girls play. They began to call this ghost Manny. Roger and Carolyn would have been hard pushed to believe the girls' crazy claims were genuine if they hadn't seen the ghosts for themselves.

Other weird occurrences began to happen soon after. Beds would occasionally float a few inches above the ground. Furniture looked to have their own thoughts, sliding over the floors on their own. As picture frames often fell off the walls, doors would open and bang shut. Roger and Carolyn gradually learned more about the house's history, which was far worse than they could have anticipated.

Prior to the Perron family, eight generations had resided on the Arnold Estate, and many of them had met with tragic ends. Mrs. John Arnold, the family's ninety-three-year-old matriarch, hanged herself in the property's barn in the late 18th century. She was only one of several suicides that occurred on the property. Prudence Arnold, eleven, was raped and killed in the house by a farmhand, while her relative, Johnny, committed suicide by hanging himself in the attic. There were also two drownings in a stream that flowed through the estate throughout the years, as well as the deaths of four men who inexplicably froze on the grounds some years earlier.

Despite this bleak past, the Perron family found solace in the fact that all of the ghosts they had encountered in the home had been helpful. That is, until the other spirits of Arnold Estate made their presence known.

Late at night, the girls saw an unwanted visitor in their beds. While they slept, an unseen entity would tug on their legs and hair. One spirit began to torture Cindy, eight, by repeatedly telling her that there were dead soldiers buried in the walls.

There is one ghost that the Perron family refuses to discuss in great detail, despite all of the family's otherworldly encounters. Andrea Perron, who published a book about her family's experiences in the house, suggested that the ghost assaulted her and her sisters. That apparition, however, was not the only bad ghost that stayed in the house. The Arnold Estate was plagued by a spirit known as Bathsheba.

According to local tradition, Bathsheba Thayer married Judson Sherman in the mid-1800s and later moved to the Old Arnold Estate. Bathsheba was charged with murder when the union's first child died. A sharp instrument had impaled the infant's skull, and the townspeople murmured that the murder had been committed as a sacrifice to Satan, and that Bathsheba was a practicing Satanist who had summoned the Devil to bestow her the gift of beauty. She was detained but released soon after owing to a lack of evidence. She remained in the house for the rest of her life as an outcast from the town, dying in the early twentieth century by hanging herself from a tree behind the house. Her body is reported to have magically turned to stone after she died.

Bathsheba and her husband did, in fact, dwell in the house, according to public record. She was also implicated in the death of her neighbor's baby child, who had been left in her care, though no trial was ever held. Bathsheba and Judson Sherman died in the

1880s and spent their final years at the old Arnold Estate. She was laid to rest in a local Baptist cemetery, where her gravestone may still be located.

Bathsheba's specter, on the other hand, loomed big for the Perron family. They were sure that her malevolent soul lingered on the land, intent on tormenting anybody who set foot on it. Every member of the Perron family saw her, her face gray and her head twisted to one side as if her neck had been permanently broken. Nonetheless, it became obvious that the creature was particularly interested in Carolyn, her least favorite person in the home.

Initially, these assaults were minor. Carolyn felt small pinches on her flesh or was smacked by an unidentified hand. Bathsheba began to hurl various items at Carolyn anytime she was caught off guard. However, things continued to deteriorate. Carolyn was sitting on the couch one day when a searing ache went up to her leg. She checked herself and discovered a puncture hole on her leg that was already bleeding.

The wound appeared to have been caused by a sewing needle. Bathsheba attempted to possess Carolyn when these attacks failed to get her to leave the residence.

Roger Perron and his daughters were desperate for assistance and called Ed and Lorraine Warren. The famed paranormal investigators were already well-known for their work on instances such as the infamous Amityville house haunting. Carolyn was tossed around the room like a ragdoll, and the Warrens and Perrons stared in terror as she talked to them in a foreign voice. The Warrens decided to provide a hand and set out to rid the house of all evil.

Later on, the Perrons desired nothing more than to leave Arnold Estate, but they could not do so due to financial difficulties. They suffered the number of ghosts in the house for ten long years until they were financially able to move in 1980. Today, paranormal enthusiasts are kindly urged to respect the present owners' privacy and stay away from the property; perhaps they are afraid of reawakening the ghosts.

6.The Defeo Family (Amityville Horror)

This is nearly completely due to the 1977 novel The Amityville Horror, subsequently adapted into a film series. Despite the book's claim that it recounts the "actual narrative" of the hauntings that occurred within its walls, there is evidence that the inhabitants of 112 Ocean Avenue – George and Kathy Lutz – made up the story that became an urban legend.

The horrific killings that occurred in the mansion before the Lutz's tenancy, on the other hand, were not manufactured. Six members of the DeFeo family were murdered in their sleep with a.35 caliber rifle on November 13, 1974.

Ronald "Butch" DeFeo Jr., the eldest kid, admitted to murdering his whole family in cold blood at 23. Louise and Ronald DeFeo Sr. and his siblings 18-year-old Dawn, 13-year-old Allison, 12-year-old Marc, and nine-year-old John Matthew were all killed.

The heinous Amityville killings are thought to have triggered the spirits that haunt 112 Ocean Avenue.

Some claim, however, that the DeFeo family was also a victim of the home.

So, did an evil presence already inhabit the home before the Amityville killings, compelling a young man to murder his whole family?

Ronald DeFeo Jr.'s upbringing was financially secure but not content. His father was a dominating and abusive guy, and his mother seemed to recede into the background due to his dominant nature. Ronald DeFeo Jr. became increasingly disturbed as he matured into his adolescence. To cope, he began to rely on narcotics and booze. He retaliated aggressively and threatened his father with a pistol. DeFeo's parents believed that a weekly stipend and gifts would satisfy their difficult son. Ronald had a job at the family-owned auto business at 18, but he rarely showed there.

So it was not unusual for DeFeo to leave work at noon on that day in 1974 out of boredom. He went to a pub with pals, continually phoning his house, getting no answer, and whining to anybody who would listen. Eventually, he departed. The next time anybody saw Ronnie, Amityville would be permanently changed.

According to Valrie Plaza's book, DeFeo returned to the bar about 6:30 a.m., shouting, "You had to assist me!" "I believe my mum and father have been assassinated!" Some customers followed him back to the residence on Ocean Avenue, where they witnessed the terrible sight inside.

All six victims were discovered in their beds, on their stomachs. At about 3:15 a.m., the victims seemed to have been shot with a high-powered rifle. The victim is Ronald Jr.'s parents, Ronald DeFeo Sr. and Louise DeFeo, as well as his four siblings, Dawn, Allison, Marc, and John Matthew, who were killed. All of the victims were shot about three o'clock in the morning using a.35 caliber lever action Marlin 336C rifle. Both

DeFeo's parents had been shot twice, while all of the children had been murdered with single shots. According to physical evidence, Louise DeFeo and her daughter Allison were both conscious at the time of their deaths. The victims were discovered face down in bed, according to Suffolk County Police. The DeFeo family had owned 112 Ocean Avenue since 1965. The six victims were eventually interred at Farmingdale's Saint Charles Cemetery.

However, there were a few things that didn't makeup. There were no indications of a fight or proof that they had been drugged on the corpses. No waking neighbors reported hearing any gunshots, only the DeFeo family dog barking into the night. Following an inquiry, Ronald DeFeo's alibi of being at work and then the bar began to crack, as investigators discovered the family had died before 6 a.m. DeFeo hurriedly altered his narrative, as he did numerous times throughout the inquiry into the Amityville killings.

At one point, he claimed that mob hitman Louis Falini murdered his family and forced DeFeo to see it. However, Falini had a good out-of-state alibi, and DeFeo quickly confessed to police what was thought to be the truth: he murdered his family on his own.

On October 14, 1975, DeFeo went on trial. His attorney, William Weber, filed an insanity plea on his behalf, claiming that the defendant heard voices telling him to kill his family.

On the other hand, the prosecution contended that while the drug-addicted DeFeo was disturbed, he understood exactly what he was doing when he committed the Amityville murders. A jury found him guilty on six counts of second-degree murder and sentenced him to six consecutive terms ranging from 25 years to life in prison.

In a later version of Ronald DeFeo Jr.'s altered narrative, he claims that his sister Dawn murdered their father, and then their heartbroken mother murdered all of the siblings. DeFeo only killed his mother in this scenario. Then, in another version told by DeFeo in 1990, Dawn shoots all the DeFeos before he kills Dawn. Other hypotheses suggest that there was a second gunman in the house.

Though the legends of the Amityville house being haunted are debatable, there is considerable doubt that Ronald DeFeo Jr. was there for his family's horrific murder at the house. But the question of whether the Amityville home is indeed haunted remains unanswered.

Whether you think the Amityville home is haunted or not, there is still some intriguing material available. Daniel Lutz, one of their kids, claimed to have possessed a spirit similar to Regan MacNeil in The Exorcist. Their second son, Christopher, is adamant that he has had encounters with the paranormal, including a time when he saw a presence "as definite as a shadow" in the figure of a man that walked toward him and then vanished.

Surprisingly, both George and Kathy Lutz passed a lie detector exam concerning their tale.

7.Exorcism of Michael Taylor

Christina Taylor   Michael Taylor

Michael Taylor (born about 1944) rose to prominence in England in 1974 due to the Ossett murder case and his purported demonic possession. The case received significant coverage in the British media. Although some contend that he was not possessed, Taylor was sent to a mental institution because his wicked intentions were not hallucinatory.

Taylor worked as a butcher in Ossett, West Yorkshire. Taylor's wife, Christine, told a Christian Fellowship Group to which Taylor joined in 1974 that his connection with the group's lay leader, Marie Robinson, was "carnal." Robinson herself told the group that Taylor was a "satanist," and he was excommunicated from the group in October 1976. On November 1, 1973, Taylor was convicted of assaulting his wife with an iron bar. He served only nine months of his sentence after claiming that his wife had attacked him first.

Taylor began to attend an evangelical Christian Bible study group at Ossett Baptist Church run by Marie

Robinson in 1974 and began working with Robinson in her telemarketing business, Joseph Enterprises Ltd., at Ossett in 1976. Michael Taylor acknowledged to feeling wicked within himself and finally verbally assaulted Robinson, who shouted back at him. Michael Taylor obtained an absolution at the following meeting, but his behavior proceeded to become increasingly unpredictable. Consequently, the local vicar summoned other ministers skilled in deliverance to cast out the demons dwelling within the guy.

The Exorcism, which took place on the 5–6 October 1974 at St. Thomas's Church in Gawber, was led by Father Peter Vincent, the Anglican Priest of St. Thomas's, and assisted by the Rev. Raymond Smith, a Methodist clergyman. The Exorcism was recorded on videotape, with the explicit permission and encouragement of Michael Taylor. The tape is now in possession of Michael Taylor's family (and has been digitized).

Exorcism was successful in that it apparently drove the possessing entity away. After the Exorcism, Michael Taylor returned to work and lived a relatively normal life. He retired in December 1991, after which re-emergence of symptoms led to his being committed to a mental hospital in 1992, where he remained until his death early in 1998 (the actual date is unclear). Father Michael Maginot performed the last Exorcism on August 24 1995.According to Bill Ellis, a modern cultural expert on folklore and the occult, the exorcists thought they had: "During an all-night ritual, at least forty demons, including those of incest, bestiality, blasphemy, and lewdness, were called and cast out. Finally, weary, they let Taylor go home, despite their belief that at least three devils remained in him: insanity, murder, and violence."

Michael Taylor viciously murdered his wife, Christine, when she was at home. He assaulted her with his bare hands, pulling out her eyes and tongue and nearly ripping her face off, before murdering their dog. A police officer discovered him nude in the street, covered in blood.

Taylor was acquitted on the basis of insanity in his March trial. He was committed to Broadmoor Hospital for two years before being transferred to a security ward in Bradford for another two years before being freed. The unusual character of the case drew a lot of attention.

Taylor made headlines again in July 2005 after being convicted guilty of indecently touching a teenage girl. A week into his jail sentence for the killing, Taylor – who had tried suicide four times in the years before the conviction – resumed showing the odd behavior that had preceded his wife's death in 1974. When he was brought back before the court, they ordered him to get psychiatric treatment once more.

8.Exorcism of Clara Germana Cele

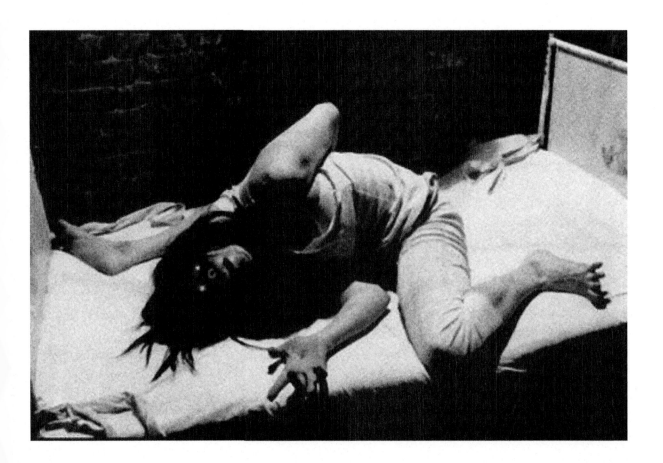

Clara Germana Cele was 16 years old when she was discovered to be possessed by an evil spirit. It is strongly suspected that he previously made a pact with the spirit. Clara was an orphan of African descent who had been baptized as a child. The girl made a pact with Satan when she was sixteen, which is the cause of her demonic possession. Clara later told her confessor, Father Hörner Erasmus, about this knowledge. According to a nun's account, Clara was said to be able to speak languages she had never heard of before. Others attest that she "understood Polish, German, French, Norwegian, and all other languages." According to the nun, Clara exhibited clairvoyance by revealing the most intimate secrets and transgressions of people she had no contact with.

Furthermore, Clara was unable to tolerate the presence of blessed objects and appeared to be imbued with extraordinary strength and ferocity, frequently hurling nuns around the convent rooms and beating them up. According to the nun, the girl's cries had a savage bestiality that astounded those around her.

According to all accounts, Clara was a very normal, even shy kid who was as devout and pious as her friends. There would have been no sign at the time that anything was wrong with her, or that evil forces were gathering about her like storm clouds on a bright day, and certainly, no indication that this beautiful young girl would go on to become one of the scariest demonic possession cases on record.

The majority of what is known about the case comes from notebooks and diaries written by nuns and priests at the mission. While it is unknown when the episode began, it appears likely that it began with a confession Clara made one day. She supposedly informed her confessor, Father Hörner Erasmus, that she had called out to the Devil to establish a dark alliance, but she did not elaborate on why she had done so. However, soon following this revelation, a sequence of odd events would begin to orbit the girl.

Clara, who knew no other languages, began to talk in Polish, German, French, Latin, and other languages, beginning with a few words here and there and then progressing to complete phrases and even raving. She had never shown any talent or even an interest in these languages, leaving everyone confused and a bit concerned that she should now know them to any degree. Clara, too, said she had no idea how she was able to speak these languages. Many others at the mission observed this. It was also stated that these periods of speaking foreign languages frequently occurred after Clara fell into a type of stupor or trance. She would sometimes not even recall what she had spoken of what had happened to her during these spells.

Soon after, Clara progressed to impulsively spewing forth the deepest, darkest secrets of others around her, including horrible things they had done and dirty thoughts they had had. She reveled in the most heinous sexual fantasies she said the members of the cloth around her had, many of which were corroborated in journal entries by terrified nuns who believed Clara could read their minds. She seemed to know all of their concerns and numerous other bits of knowledge she had no right to know, and it was at this time, everyone realized something very weird was going on.

Clara began to develop an aversion to religious images in the days that followed, which must have been difficult given that she was on a Christian mission. She would take circuitous routes around these things and couldn't stand being in the same room with them.

During these episodes, it was reported that Clara would gain tremendous strength, toss nuns across the room, and be unable to be restrained even by four people. Clara's overall propensity to progressively shift from a previously quiet and even shy adolescent to a more assertive, strong, and combative personality corresponded with this. She would hiss, snarl, and growl at everyone around her, most of the time unprovoked, and the increasingly terrified nuns sought assistance in performing an exorcism on what they were now sure was a demon-possessed kid.

Rev. Mansueti and Rev. Erasmus, two Roman Catholic priests, went about executing an exorcism on Clara, which proved to be a frightening ordeal. When faced with the two, the girl sprang onto Rev. Mansueti, knocked away his bible, and began strangling him with his stole, and she would have succeeded if a group of nuns and the other Priest hadn't pulled her off of him. After that, she started throwing items around and allegedly levitated a full 5 feet of the floor, forcing those there to have her restrained.

For two days, the priests faced whatever demonic evil was living within Clara. During it all, she demonstrated numerous characteristics that convinced everyone there that she was not just a mentally sick kid or crazy. She seemed to know when she was being sprayed with holy water, in addition to levitation and speaking in tongues. To put this to the test, the priests swapped between holy water and plain water without Clara's knowledge, but while regular water had no impact, holy water drove her insane. However, it appears that the holy water was the key, which ultimately threw the demon out.

The case is obscure and poorly recorded, yet it is unquestionably strange and was observed by many individuals. Various witnesses saw this teenager exhibit classic signs of demonic possession, including speaking in languages they have no business knowing, aversion to religious paraphernalia, superhuman strength, uncharacteristic violent behavior if the reports are to be believed. According to some, the girl levitated five feet in the air, sometimes vertically, sometimes horizontally; when sprinkled with holy water, she is claimed to have come out of her diabolical possession. They may all be telling the truth, but why would they? How can one explain these events if they are caused by mental illness? There is no way of knowing if demonic possession is true in the literal sense, but the case of Clara Germana Cele undoubtedly rates among the most potentially authentic reports available.

According to a Lutheran Pastoral Handbook, these signs indicate that a person is possessed rather than suffering from a mental disease. As a result, two Roman Catholic priests, Rev. Mansueti (Director of the St. Michael's Mission) and Rev. Erasmus (her confessor) were assigned to execute an exorcism on Clara Germana Cele lasted two days. Clara's initial move during the Exorcism was to knock the Holy Bible from the Priest's hands and grasp his stole to suffocate him with it. The Devil was claimed to have been pushed out of the girl at the end of the Exorcism.

9.The Smurl's Poltergeist

The Smurls went through hell and pure torture that no human being should have to endure. In 1972, there was a terrible hurricane that came through called hurricane Agnes. It flooded many people out of their homes, and among them were Jack and Janet Smurl. They had several children and a pet German Shepherd by the name of Simon. Because of the flood, they had to look for another place to live, and that is how they moved into a that was located at 328 chase Street in West Pitts in Pennsylvania.

They moved into the home in 1973 with their parents, so Jack's parents, by the name of John and Mary, moved to the other side of the duplex. A duplex is a house that's kind of split into two so that people can live on one side some people can live on the other. It's similar to an apartment, but it looks like a normal house. So, Jack's family, John and Mary Smurl, moved into one side of the duplex while Jack and Janet moved into the other half with their children.

There were no issues for the first 18 months of living in the house; everything was completely fine. Though there were few occurrences here and there that had happened, but not enough to call it paranormal or cause scare to the point of making you want to move out. Though, some of the happenings at that time were a little bit odd. Since the house was built in 1896, it was backdated for the Smurfs, so they began renovating the duplex themselves, installing new floors, and doing many paintings to make it a little bit modern. But, little did they know that the next thirteen years were going to be the worst period of their lives, all because of their new home. The beginning of 1974 was like any other year until strange noises, and other odd occurrences began to disrupt the peace. As time passed, the cases became severe, and they began to experience things like the television and water pipes getting destroyed without anyone actually doing it. Later on, they started seeing apparitions and continued for the next 11 years, with each week getting worse and worse.

When the paranormal occurrences began to change rapidly for the Smurls, really dark, violent things started happening there. Initially, they kept it secret and didn't come out about it for several years to come, but everything got so bad that they ended up actually coming out to the public about it in the 80s in an effort to seek help. By that time, they were scared for their lives; the darkest of things you could imagine occurs in a haunted house was what was happening there. In the summer of 1986, the family decided to come public about what had been happening in their home since 1974.

The haunted attacks: Let's begin with a very large ceiling fan falling from their ceiling randomly and almost landing on one of their daughters, Shannon, and almost killing her. They were all excited about going to the Church for their daughter's confirmation rite when the fan above started to shake, tore itself loose, and almost hit the girl. After this incidence came to the ghostly attacks and disturbances of which they were repeatedly attacked by what they believe to be a demonic entity inside of their home. One of the daughters said that she would be lying in her bed on repeated occasions, and she could actually see what looked like people, really creepy people floating in her bedroom like above her bed, while she was trying to sleep.

Not long after that, the odor came; they started smelling something terrible in their house almost constantly and related the odor to that of rotten flesh. They said it was horrible sometimes, you wouldn't smell anything, and then suddenly, this wave of rotten flesh would just overtake their entire house. It was all that they could smell (Imagine if you were about to dig into your favorite meal, and that happened). The ghostly attacks got so bad that there was one night that Janet and Jack were actually intimate in their bedroom, and Janet was violently pushed off of her bed in the middle of the activity with her husband. He was left on the bed by himself, gagging from the smell. I'd say that that's some jealous ghost.

That wasn't the first time somebody was physically lifted up and thrown or levitated off something. It was claimed that they were levitated off of their beds on multiple occasions and even said that their dog, Simon, was picked up and thrown into a wall. Jack said that there was one night that he was praying. There had been a lot of activity in the house that night, and he was actually pulled off the bed and dragged across the floor

The slaps: Still on the ghost attacks, several family members in this house got slapped by absolutely nothing. They felt as if a hand hit them and said that sometimes when they would feel this and turn around to see what it was, they would see these dark shadows just hovering around. This happened multiple times, and it wasn't like a random slap and not finding out who did it. It happened to many people in the family several times, and it was always accompanied by this just really dark shadow.

Electricity and plumbing problems: prior to the ghosts, the lights would turn on and off, doors would open and close, drawers would even open and close. They said that one of their TVs actually burst into flames, among other electrical problems. They also had many problems with their pipes since they were remodeling the house; their toilets would randomly flush by themselves. There were animal claw-like scratches on the bathtubs and so on. On multiple occasions, they would hear what sounded like somebody scratching violently on the walls or on the floor, even if no one was there. They also heard their names being called on several occasions, like when one of their daughters, Janet, would go down into the basement to do the wash and she heard somebody who sounded like their mother calling "Janet, Janet..." and she would reply only to realize that she wasn't there.

After a decade of psychological torture, the family called Annette and Lorraine Warren. By then, the Warrens were already known for their work. Their investigation led to an obvious conclusion there were lots of evil presences, but one demon was in control, and what was most frightening was the fact that a passageway between two dimensions was located in the house. This could be the reason for the haunting. The Warrens tried everything from exorcisms to antagonizing whatever was there, but nothing seems to work. The house was now under full possession, with people being constantly attacked violently, intensifying every time the family was starting to lose hope and thought they were doomed to live in damnation. But, after the fourth and final Exorcism, things became better after moving out of the residence, and the family had complete relief in 1986. The peace they had experienced so long ago had finally returned to them; however, the family would never be the same again.

10. The Tanacu Exorcism of Maricica Irina Cornici

Maricica Irina Cornici, a supposedly mentally ill nun from the Romanian Orthodox Church of Tanacu in the County of Vaslui, Romania, was declared murdered by the Exorcism led by Priest Daniel Petre Corogeanu and four Orthodox Christian nuns of the Holy Trinity order. The story was widely reported in Romanian media. Following a long trial, the Priest was sentenced to seven years in appeal, one nun to six, and another three nuns to five years. However, many of the locals of Tanacu, including Cornici's brother, felt she had suffered from demonic possession. The coroner Dan Gheorghiu claimed that an overdose of adrenaline in the ambulance caused the nun's death.

Maricica Irina Cornici, 23, moved to the Tanacu Monastery in January 2005. She was born into a broken home. She and her brother grew up in the orphanage following the suicide of her father. When she was 19, she worked in Germany as a nanny, then in Banat for a family. An orphanage friend of hers became a nun in the Tanacu monastery, who encouraged her to become a nun too. She started chuckling at Mass shortly after, and by April, her mental state had deteriorated to the point where doctors at the local psychiatric institution diagnosed her with schizophrenia. After two weeks of therapy, she was released into the monastery care. Cornici's friends reportedly claimed she never showed signs of mental illness. Her brother testified that he was with her when he saw Satan going "to her" and said she had been diabolically possessed.

Daniel Petre Corogeanu was the monastery's 29-year-old Priest. A decade before the events, in Vaslui, his native town, he was a soccer player. After being denied admittance to the University of Bucharest, where he planned to study sports or law, he began theological studies at the University of Iași. One year later, a businessman recruited him from his hometown to help establish a monastery bordering the town. He had been ordained by the local bishop, who expected his studies to continue. However, he gave up his academic study to dedicate himself to the administration of the monastery.

Father Corogeanu had differences with the diocese in 2003. When the bishop came to read him the law of the Canon, he contended that the Freemasonry regulations were "innovations of the 19th century." The initial community of monks disbanded as they became priests and, instead, Corogeanu created a community of religious nuns "totally devoted to him," according to all reports.

Father Corogeanu believed that Cornici was possessed by Satan, not only a mental condition. He further claimed that "the devil can't be taken out of humans with medications," so Exorcism existed. To prevent her from violent movements, including those that struck her, she was confined by the nuns in her bedroom as they took part in the ritual of the Ascension of Jesus. A few days later, with their arms held out, they bound her to a cross and took her inside the Church to anoint her. According to Sr. Nicoleta Arcalianu, Cornici was confined in the same way as others possessed by demons; Sr. Arcalianus added that if she hadn't restrained Cornici, she 'might have murdered herself or killed anyone else.' Sister Arcalianu said, with relation to Cornici, 'Irina knew she had evil spirits since she asked us to tie her together and help her.'

Her wrists and forehead were then salvaged with holy oil and remained three days in the Church. They placed a cloth in her mouth that prevented her from cursing and prayed to throw the Devil out as they bathed her lips with holy water. Cornici was then taken and untied in her room. According to Father Corogeanu, she was "healed." Later on, she had bread and tea and fainted after she had eaten. The nuns couldn't get her up and felt her pulse was faint and phoned an ambulance. She was given six doses of adrenaline in the ambulance, but she was dead when she arrived at the hospital.

The hospital doctors contacted the police, who saw the marks left by the shackles on both wrists and knees.

An autopsy from 2005 claimed that she died of dehydration, tiredness, and oxygen deficiency.

Father Corogeanu and the four religious who supported him were accused of murder and the deprivation of freedom. The Prosecutors sought a life sentence for Corogeanu but were convicted to 14 years imprisonment in 2007 and 5-8 years' imprisonment on the nuns (Nicoleta Arcalianu, Adina Cepraga, Elena Otel, and Simona Bandanas). Many people were present in the courtroom to support Father Corogeanu and were disturbed by the judgment. The Court of Appeal decreased his sentence to 7 years, and in November 2011,Corogeanu was released after completing two-thirds of his sentence.

During Marice Irina Cornici's burial, "the claps of thunder were heard," and Corogeanu concluded, "that the will of God was done."

The monastery was closed down by the Romanian Orthodox Church, and Corogeanuwas excommunicated.

However, it was discovered in 2014 that the cause of death was due to an overdose of adrenaline administered in the ambulance; as Coroner Dan Gheorghiustated, 'I was a member of the team in charge of the exhumation of the nun's body.' The conclusion was that an excess of adrenaline killed the woman. Don't ask me, and I don't know why the judges didn't consider it." According to Fr. Corogeanu, "My biggest blunder was calling an ambulance when I noticed she wasn't moving. I suppose she is dead because she was given too much adrenaline by the doctors who came with the ambulance. If I didn't call the ambulance, she'd be OK now."

In Tanacu, many people still claim that Cornici was possessed rather than mentally ill, and Corogeanu did his best to help her. Veronica Tomulescu said, "It's not like they killed her. They didn't stab her or shoot her. They took her alive to the hospital."

11. Nicole Aubrey's Possession

Nicole Aubrey (sometimes spelt Obry) was a married young girl who began experiencing bodily torments in November 1565, which she said were caused by a vision of her deceased grandfather. Nicole, a fifteen-year-old resident of Vervins, France, had gotten so ill that she couldn't eat and allegedly went into such contortions that, as one eyewitness subsequently described, twelve or fifteen men were required to hold her down. She also talked in a harsh and scary tone, claiming that her grandfather's ghost controlled her. The grandpa said that he died without confessing and that as a result, Nicole and her family were required to perform different penances. Despite the family's efforts to comply, the possession persisted.

Nicole's family arranged for an exorcism to be performed by a Dominican priest, Pierre de la Motte. De la Motte persuaded the possessed spirit that it was a devil rather than an angel through numerous exorcisms. Nicole's possession worsened, and she became deaf, blind, and deafeningly (to make her unable to take communion). In addition, the principal devil who possessed her allegedly encouraged a slew of other devils to come in and inhabit her body. According to accounts, de la Motte expelled twenty-eight of Nicole's demons, following which they "fled to Geneva" (which was the centre of the Calvinist movement at the time). The principal demon that possessed her called himself "Beelzebub, the Prince of the Huguenots". Huguenots were French Protestants), insisted that no one could force him out save the Bishop of Laon. When Bishop Jean de Bours came to Vervins in January 1566 to perform an exorcism, he had no better luck than the other priests.

The issue rapidly became political, with local Huguenots arguing that the entire possession tale was a fabrication and attempting to halt the exorcisms. They had cause to be sceptical, given that "Beelzebub" was accusing them of collaborating with Satan. Nicole was transported to Laon, mostly for her own safety, where she was subjected to a series of public exorcisms with all the grandeur of a religious spectacle. Nicole was carried in a huge religious procession from the monastery where she resided to the beautiful Cathedral Notre-Dame de Laon, where she ascended a specially built scaffold. The exorcist would instruct "Prince Beelzebub" to appear in front of a huge crowd, and Nicole would obediently deliver a lecture on the atrocities that the Protestants would wreak on France's Catholics. The substance was like the anti-Huguenot sermons delivered regularly by priests and bishops across the country.

The fact that a demon, one of Satan's fallen angels, was telling Catholics who were hearing what they most wanted to believe about their Huguenot neighbours seemed certain to exacerbate religious tensions. "Prince Beelzebub," told his audience, among other things, that local Huguenots had taken a communion wafer, sliced it up, and burnt the fragments. "Beelzebub" also bragged, "I will do Him [Christ] more damage than the Jews did!"

"The Catholics in great pleasure offered praises to God, being more confirmed in their faith," one Catholic chronicler wrote of Nicole Aubrey's public exorcisms. "While some Huguenots returned to the road of salvation, others became more and more obstinate, ridiculing the entire ensuing affair." The fact that Huguenots maintained that the entire event was a deception performed by the Church employing a naïve little girl did nothing to alleviate tensions. The "miracle of Laon" happened on February 8, 1566, when the Bishop of Laon held up a communion wafer and drove out the last of Nicole's demons. Nicole appears to have slipped into obscurity after that since nothing further appears to have been documented about her.

The "miracle" of Laon helped to cement anti-Protestant views, with Catholic clergy disseminating the news across Europe to become one of the Counter-rallying Reformation's grounds. It was also crucial in the religious holy wars that raged in France throughout the 16th century. This includes the St. Bartholomew's

Day Massacre in August 1572, which resulted in the deaths of thousands of Huguenots. The French Wars of Religion would last until the end of the 16th century, culminating in the expulsion of the Huguenots from France.

One of the most interesting aspects of Nicole's possession was her ability to communicate without the use of her vocal cords. Jean Boulaese, the author of the most well-known account of Nicole and her possession:

Speaking in Nicole, with her mouth open wide enough to allow a walnut to pass through and swelling beneath the throat; or, to be more precise, beneath the chin; but in any case, without using or moving the lips, the grandfather replied loudly in a cracked voice: I am from God, who endured death and suffering for us all, from the virgin Mary, and all the saints of Pentecost. I am Joachim Willot's soul.

Nicole first maintained that her grandfather's spirit was using her body with her conscious participation, but she was subsequently obliged to alter this to conform to Catholic theology. Because theology did not permit the idea of "good spirits" using living humans to transmit messages, their interrogation moulded her replies to conform with Church teachings on demonic possession. Given her eagerness to please her interrogators, the anti-Protestant message she conveyed does not come as a surprise.

Nicole Aubrey's possession was important in terms of spawning copycat cases of possession, in addition to fueling the anti-Huguenot frenzy engulfing France. In 1582, four individuals were publicly exorcised in the French city of Soissons. One of these, a 13-year-old child called Laurent, was said to have been possessed by a demon known as Bonsoir. Another possessed stood out because he was a 50-year-old guy who had been possessed twice (repossessed?). A third instance was even more unique since it included a lady called

Marguerite Obry (not related), who claimed to be possessed by the same Beelzebub who had previously possessed Nicole Aubrey.

Though the Soissons' belongings were never as well-known as Nicole Aubry's, there were many parallels. When holy relics were placed on their stomachs or forced to drink holy water, all possessions fell into convulsions. They also charged the local Huguenots with numerous religious offences, as Nicole Aubrey did. The demons allegedly claimed to have come to "comfort their Huguenot pals" but were compelled to acknowledge the might of the True Church during the public Exorcism that drove them away.

After hearing about Nicole Aubrey's case, Marthe Brossier, the last famous possession case of the 16th century, allegedly became convinced that she was possessed. Marthe's family transported her from town to town in the Loire valley beginning in 1598, when she had several public exorcisms. This went on for nearly a year before French officials detained her for fear of inciting anti-Huguenot hatred. Marthe either fled (or was assisted in escaping) and resumed her search for exorcisms, this time in southern France. Despite her trip to Rome and appeals to the Vatican, Marthe was diagnosed with sickness rather than being possessed.

Though the period of possession was far from finished, the Nicole Aubrey exorcism and others like it became a major plank in the Catholic Church's propaganda battle against Protestant movements. The "miracle of Laon" would live on in Catholic tradition long after the political upheaval that inspired it had subsided. The fact that Exorcism and incidents of demonic possession are still practised in many countries today indicates its usefulness as a technique for bolstering belief systems challenged by criticism. The effectiveness of that technique is determined by people's willingness to believe the unbelievable.

12. Elizabeth Knapp (The Groton Witch)

Elizabeth Knapp was born in 1655 in Massachusetts. When she was 16, she worked as a servant for Reverend Samuel Willard of Groton, Massachusetts, when she began to show indications of being possessed by the Devil.

Reverend Willard noticed that when her symptoms worsened – she had severe fits, complained of being strangled, and attempted to hurl herself into the fire. She began to "carry herself in a weird and unwelcome manner," saw apparitions and had violent "fits" for three months.

During one of her fits, she talked in a "hollow" voice and referred to the minister as "a huge black rogue" who "tell[s] the people a company of falsehoods." "Satan, thou are a liar and a deceiver, and God will vindicate His truth one day," Willard said. Others in the room joined in the fight, informing the Devil that "God had him in chains."

The response was, "For all my chain, I can hit thee in the head whenever I choose." Meanwhile, Elizabeth said that the Devil had promised to turn her into a "witch" if she signed a "contract" to become his servant in her voice.

Events in Groton proceeded on the idea that Satan entices some individuals to enter into a contract with him, assuring them, as he told Elizabeth Knapp, that everything "shall be fine." They no longer have to be concerned about sin and salvation. The inhabitants of Groton likewise believed that good would triumph over evil in the whole course of God's providence.

As the tale of Elizabeth Knapp illustrates, certain difficulties sprang from Puritanism's religious demands. One expectation was that Christians perform their moral obligations to the best of their abilities. Another need was that people analyze their reasons to see whether they had adequately repented of sin and placed their whole confidence in Christ's compassion.

Reverend Willard's

Elizabeth respected the guy who served as both her Priest and her master when she wasn't possessed. When the demons were in her, though, she was vehemently opposed to him. She screamed at him, calling him a liar. She chastised her father and others for paying attention to him; questioned his authority in society and his control over her.

She had reason to dislike him. He was a young, well-off, Harvard-educated clergyman with a promising future. She was a young lady with little education and minor prospects other than servitude to others, whether as a servant, a daughter, or a wife.

He spent most of his free time reading, writing, and travelling. She had never been taught to write, seldom left Groton, and spent her time washing his house, caring for his children, bringing in his wood, and keeping his fires going - all so he could work in peace and comfort.

Puritan America was not the only place where witches were hunted. It happened in both Catholic and Protestant sections of Europe, and the toll in New England was considerably lower than in Scotland or portions of France and Germany. It's unclear why witch-hunting became lethal in certain Puritan villages but not others. Elizabeth Knapp was not a witch in any way. She married Samuel Scripture and lived a nice Puritan wife and mother's life. She was so adept at erasing her dissatisfaction that she nearly totally vanishes from public records after 1673.

Conclusion:

The answer to the forever question, "Is the paranormal real or just fiction?" hasn't been more obvious as many strange things happen around us all the time; things that, to the ordinary eye, one would say are impossible or absurd. For example, if you look at the ordeals, the Smurls had to go through, that alone is enough to stamp a big "No" on any thoughts of relocating to a house with an unknown history or origins, but almost every day, people are migrating to new unknown locations. Furthermore, what of the cases of demonic possessions misdiagnosed as mental illness? In the world today, the contents of the medical thesaurus about diseases and other forms of illnesses keep growing, and it has reached a stage where there is hardly an ailment that doesn't have a medical term ascribed to it.

On the issue of Exorcism, though, I find it quite disturbing that very few victims of demonic possessions survive the process. The whole point of finding a cure or solution for misfortune is not to die during the treatment process or right after. The essence of the whole process is to survive the treatment process, get well, and move on with life. Anything different only states the obvious that the remedy didn't work or that the tendency to live through an exorcism and come out on top is very slim. If that's the case, then it'll be easy to stick to an incurable medical term. But then, I guess the demons won't leave without putting up a fight with the host and exorcist, and since we all are different, there is no exact point that we can use as a threshold for how much pressure and torment all humans can withstand. The exorcists may not know the extent to which they are to push the body, and if that limit is exceeded, then more often than not, it leads to a sad ending that takes us to the next issue.

The deaths of the demon-possessed victims are always pinned on the exorcists and their assistants. It's almost like a trend following the victim's death and more like an avenue for people who have contradicting beliefs to devour the accused. Like any other frontline worker, they are tasked with controlling the incidence or spread of demonic possessions, which by now should be convincing to anyone in prior disbelief of its existence. These exorcists should receive accolades for volunteering to do the dirty work of freeing souls tormented here on earth because the victims, as much as we can blame the demons, can be the sources of their predicaments. While some victims are innocent and unfortunately get pulled into some circumstances, some people purposely didn't let their sleeping dogs lie by looking for these demons from some discoveries or research or ignorantly participating in rituals that provoked the deities or demons. So, if you look at it, some of the exorcists get unfair treatment because doctors don't get arrested and dragged to court for a surgery gone wrong, so why should exorcists be punished for helping to get rid of angry, stubborn demons.

By the same Collection:

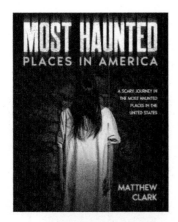

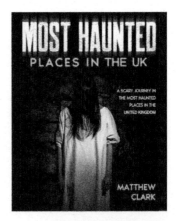

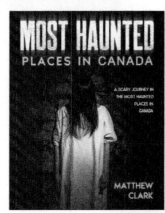

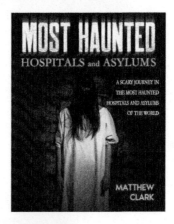

Search on Amazon!!

Printed in Great Britain
by Amazon

80361125R00061